For those who find the sunlight
—Demi

I would like to acknowledge the invaluable comments made by
Professor Elizabeth Carney, Clemson University.

A NOTE ABOUT THE BOOK

As part of the research when writing *Alexander the Great*, my son, John; his Turkish wife, Evrim Eser Hitz; and I followed in the footsteps of Alexander through Troy, Gordium, Ankara, Sardis, Pergamum, Ephesus, Magnesia, Miletus, Olympus, Phaselis, Antalya, Sidon, Side, Tarsus, Soli, and along the River Granicus. For my research, my reading included the ancient Alexander histories of Arrian, Quintus Curtius Rufus, Plutarch, Pseudo-Callisthenes, Al-Makin, and Abu Shaker, as well as *Alexander* by Theodore Ayrault Dodge (New York: Da Capo Press, 2004); *Alexander the Great in Fact and Fiction* by A.B. Bosworth (Oxford: Oxford University Press, 2002); *The History of Alexander the Great*, Vol. 1, by C. A. Robinson (Providence, RI: Brown University, 1953); *The Lost Histories of Alexander the Great* by L. C. Pearson (New York: American Philological Association, 1960); and *In the Footsteps of Alexander* by Michael Wood (Berkeley: University of California Press, 1997). For the art and architecture pictured in the artwork, I relied on many sources, including *Macedonia from Philip II to the Roman Conquest* (Princeton: Princeton University Press, 1994); *Alexander the Great: History and Legend in Art*, edited by Kate Ninou (Athens: Archaeological Receipts Fund, 1980); *Alexander the Great in Greek and Roman Art* by Margarete Bieber (Madison, WI: Argonaut Press, 1964), and many other books from my art and architecture library on Greece, Macedonia, Turkey, the Middle East, Persia, Egypt, and India.

Marshall Cavendish Corporation, 99 White Plains Road, Tarrytown, NY 10591
www.marshallcavendish.us/kids

LIBRARY OF CONGRESS CATALOGING-IN-PUBLICATION DATA: Demi. Alexander the Great / Demi. — 1st ed. p. cm. ISBN 978-0-7614-5700-8 1. Alexander, the Great, 356-323 B.C. —Juvenile literature. 2. Greece—History—Macedonian Expansion, 359-323 B.C.—Juvenile literature. 3. Generals—Greece—Biography—Juvenile literature. 4. Greece—Kings and rulers—Biography—Juvenile literature. I. Title. DF234.D46 2010 938'.07092--dc22 [B] 2009043636

The illustrations are rendered in mixed media.
Book design by Michael Nelson
Editor: Margery Cuyler
Printed in China (E)
First edition
1 3 5 6 4 2

mc Marshall Cavendish Children

ALEXANDER
THE GREAT

WITHDRAWN WRITTEN

and

ILLUSTRATED BY

Demi

MARSHALL CAVENDISH CHILDREN

ALEXANDER THE GREAT

was born on July 20, 356 BCE in Pella, the capital of Macedonia. On the night of his birth, his mother dreamed of mighty thunderbolts and his father dreamed his son would be as strong as a lion. After Alexander's birth, many said the Greek god Zeus was his father. King Philip II of Macedonia, however, was his father, and Queen Olympias his mother.

As a boy, Alexander was trained
for the life of a soldier and a king.
He learned to wrestle, throw
a javelin, scale mountains in
winter, and fight lions.

Alexander showed his bravery when his father received a gift of a huge, beautiful horse named Bucephalus. The horse was so wild and spirited that no one could ride it. Young Alexander turned the horse toward the sun so it would not be scared of its own shadow. The horse calmed down, and Alexander mounted it and rode off. King Philip II laughed and said, "Get yourself another kingdom, my boy. Macedonia's not big enough to hold you here!"

At age thirteen, Alexander was tutored by Aristotle, the greatest teacher in the land, who introduced him to science, literature, medicine, philosophy, and the importance of being compassionate to other people.

From his father, Alexander
learned about the fighting that
had been going on for years
among the Macedonians,
Persians, and Greeks.

Alexander's father had a superbly trained army. In 338 BCE, at age eighteen, Alexander led a cavalry charge into battle, helping his father conquer the Greek cities of Thebes and Athens, to bring them under Macedonian rule. King Philip II now controlled the whole Greek peninsula.

Two years later, King Philip II was assassinated at the wedding of his daughter, and Alexander became the new king.

At age twenty, Alexander was battle hardened and had the military skills to become the greatest general who ever lived.

As soon as Alexander became king, the Greeks—who had been conquered earlier during the reign of Philip II—rebelled.

Alexander quickly crushed them by fighting and winning every battle north, south, east, and west of Macedonia.

Young Alexander was determined to carry out his father's plan to conquer Persia, and so he declared war on the Persians. As he readied for battle, he consulted the oracle at Delphi. The oracle responded, "You are invincible!"

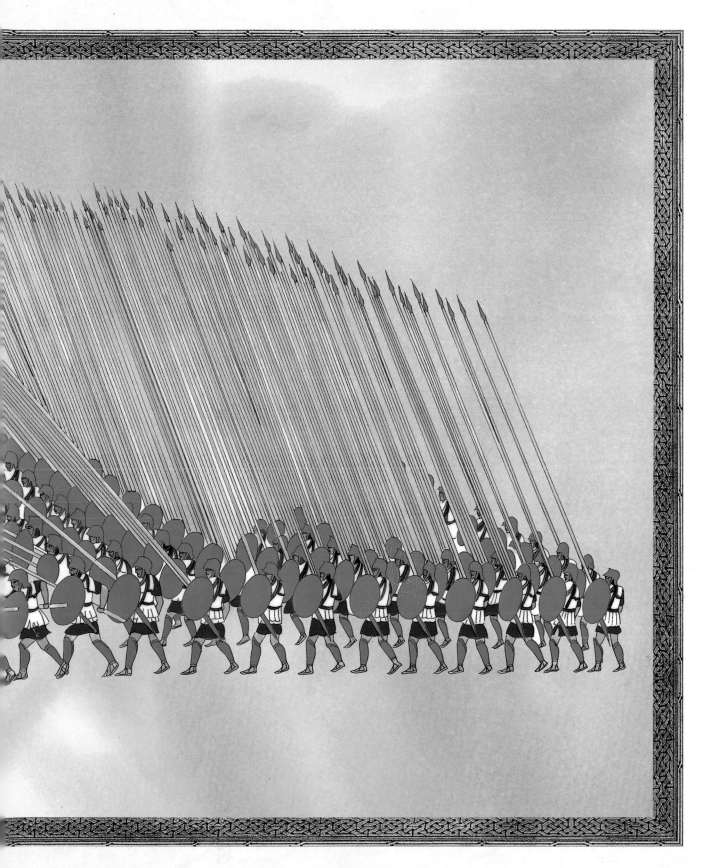

Heartened by the oracle's message, Alexander gathered 44,000 men to defeat the Persians. His infantry carried eighteen-foot-long spears. His men could fight in terrible weather on the highest mountain peaks. His archers were the best trained in the empire. His weapons included mobile siege towers, stone-throwing catapults, and javelin hurlers.

In May 334 BCE, Alexander and his army landed on the coast of Asia Minor near Troy. Driving a spear into the soil, Alexander signaled he would be victorious against the great Persian king Darius III and take all his lands.

In a surprise attack at the River Granicus, Alexander's army defeated the Persians in their heavy war chariots.

One by one, Alexander freed the Greek cities under Persian control.

On the Aegean coast at Didyma, Alexander consulted another oracle. It predicted that he would become lord of all of Asia!

Next, at Gordium, Alexander heard the strange story of the "Gordian Knot." The yoke of the ancient chariot of the first king Gordius was held in place by a knot made of bark. Whoever could undo the knot would become ruler of all of Asia. The knot's ends were invisible, so no one had ever been able to undo them. Alexander said, "It doesn't matter how the knot is untied." Drawing his sword, he hacked it open. That evening, thunder and lightning burst over Gordium, signifying that the oracle had spoken the truth.

Alexander had heard about a great Greek philosopher and mystic named Diogenes who was said to be filled with inner wisdom and light. Although Alexander had conquered many lands and was used to people humbling themselves before him, Diogenes had not visited him. If Diogenes would not come to him, Alexander would go to Diogenes!

He found Diogenes lying in his tub with the sun shining on his face. Alexander asked, "What can I do for you, sir? I have everything in the world and would do anything for you!" Diogenes laughed and said, "The only thing you can do is get out of my sunlight! I need nothing else because all that I have is within."

Alexander could feel the truth of his words. He said, "In my next life, I would not ask to be Alexander but to be Diogenes!" Diogenes said, "You do not need to wait that long. You can be Diogenes right now. Just come and sit in the sunlight with me and stop all your conquering!" Alexander replied, "First I must conquer Asia, India, and the Far East, and next I must conquer the whole world!" "Then, you will never sit with me in the light," said Diogenes. "No one returns to their inner light unless they are aware. If you are aware right this moment, the journey stops. If you are not, the journey never ends."

Alexander left. He never returned to see Diogenes, since he could not conquer himself.

In November 333 BCE, King Darius III of Persia and Alexander met on the battlefield of Issus. The Persian king was said to be the tallest and most handsome man in all of Asia. He was also considered fair and compassionate, rich, and supremely confident as commander of an enormous army.

But Alexander's swift cavalry and superior military tactics sent Darius fleeing from the battlefield. The enemy king narrowly escaped, leaving behind his royal cloak, bow, and family. The army of Darius was crushed, but Darius, a brave leader not accustomed to defeat, would later mount a new campaign against Alexander.

Next, Alexander besieged the cities of Tyre and Gaza and advanced into Egypt.

The Egyptians hated being ruled
by the Persians. They accepted
Alexander as their new leader,
particularly when he made
sacrifices to their gods.

Alexander wanted to know more about himself and his future and so he rode into the desert to consult the oracle of Zeus Ammon at Siwa. With no landmarks, his camel train traveled by the stars across barren dreary scrub, gravel beds, and burning salt wastes. Soon they lost their way and ran out of water. Surely they all would die. But, miraculously, it started to rain. Two crows appeared and guided them to Siwa. There, the high priest proclaimed Alexander the son of Zeus Ammon, master of all lands, and ruler of the whole world.

To mark this fortunate event, Alexander founded a new Egyptian city named Alexandria.

Although King Darius III and his powerful army had been defeated at the Battle of Issus, the Persian king wanted to hold onto what was left of his empire. In Babylon, he raised a new army of 500,000 troops. Their chariots were designed to mow down everything in sight.

When Alexander and his army crossed through Syria and into northern Iraq, Darius III met Alexander at Gaugamela.

The enemy's chariots proved
to be a failure, however, when
Alexander's men stepped out of
their way and killed the drivers
with arrows.

Swiftly defeated, Darius III fled,
leaving behind one hundred tons
of silver and, as before, his bow,
arrows, and chariot.

Alexander was now indeed lord
of all of Asia!

Alexander rode triumphantly
through the gates of Babylon.
He took possession of the palace,
citadel, and treasury.

Next Alexander conquered Susa and acquired one of the Persian Empire's largest stores of precious metals: 1,250 tons of gold and 225 tons of gold coins.

In the winter of 331, Alexander battled his way to Persepolis, the famous capital of Persia. He easily took the city with its palaces, ornate architecture, sculpture, paintings, and mosaics. He now possessed its enormous royal treasury of 3,000 tons of gold, while his soldiers collected a fabulous booty of silver, gold, jewelry, and priceless embroidered cloths.

That same winter Alexander took Pasargadae, the former capital of Persia. Built by Cyrus the Great, this was the place where all great kings were crowned. Alexander paid his respects to Cyrus's tomb, gaining the name "friend of Cyrus."

Next Alexander set fire to the royal palaces of Persepolis, destroying the last of the Persian Empire. Now Alexander was not only a great conqueror, he was also very rich from the spoils he had gained from all his victories.

King Darius III, meanwhile, had taken refuge in the gold and silver palace in Ecbatana. Determined to win back land and power, Darius III created a new army of 33,000 soldiers, but many of his men deserted him.

As Darius III rode beyond the Caspian Gates, Alexander and his army pursued him. Darius III could not keep his troops together, and entire units deserted to join Alexander's army.

One of Darius III's own generals arrested the Persian king and locked him up inside a horse-drawn cart. The general murdered Darius III and proclaimed himself the new great king, only later to be hunted down and defeated by Alexander.

Alexander found the body
of Darius III and carried it
back to Persepolis. He buried
his old enemy in the traditional
Persian style.

Alexander recruited Persian troops for his army because he believed that if he forged a close alliance between the Macedonians and the Persians, he could better hold onto the empire he now ruled. He began to adopt the customs of the Persian courts, placing a crown on his own head and wearing the great robes of the Persian kings.

The fact that Alexander embraced the customs of his former enemy infuriated his Greek subjects, and some of them started to rebel. Alexander used brutal means to subdue or execute anyone in his kingdom who protested.

In 328 BCE, Alexander married Roxana, the daughter of an Afghan nobleman, and later, he married one of King Darius III's daughters.

Alexander now set his sights on Afghanistan and India, conquering huge stone fortresses and mountaintop kingdoms.

He fought the greatest battle of
his life against King Porus by
the River Hydaspes.

King Porus was seven feet tall and so strong, he could hurl his javelins with the strength of a catapult. He had 300 chariots and 200 terrifying war elephants. But during the battle, Porus's many chariots got stuck in the mud. Once again, Alexander and his troops were victorious.

Alexander fought many more
bloody battles, bringing most
of India under his control.

When he reached the banks of the Hyphasis River, however, his soldiers rebelled after ten years of fighting. Alexander called his men together and desperately described new and exciting campaigns in hopes they would stay—but he was unsuccessful.

His men, weary of warfare, wanted
to return to their homeland to see
their wives and children.

Alexander had to give in, and so he turned back.

He ordered some of his men and horses to be shipped home by sea. They suffered water and food shortages, tidal waves, whale attacks, and warring armies at ports along the way. He ordered some of his army—and most of his elephants—to journey over the treacherous Himalayan mountains in the north.

He himself took a southern route through the desert with the rest of his men. It was the most grueling journey imaginable, and thousands of the soldiers died.

Finally, in January 324 BCE, Alexander marched into Persia. After being away for six years, he found his empire in serious disarray. As was his custom, he restored order by executing anyone who dared to challenge him.

He ordered a mass wedding between the Macedonians and Persians. Ten thousand Macedonian soldiers married Persian commoners. One hundred officers married Persian nobles, many of them against their will.

Alexander planned next to invade Arabia, Carthage, and Rome. In 324 BCE, he built a fleet of ships strong enough to conquer all the seas of the world and dominate the trade routes.

But his plans were interrupted when his dearest friend, Hephaestion, honored above all others, died. Alexander was so overwhelmed with sadness that he cut off his hair and the manes and tails of all his horses to show his grief. Then he erected a gigantic tomb for his great friend.

Following a banquet on June 3, 323 BCE, Alexander developed a fever. For several days, it rose and fell until on the evening of June 13, among the despairing cries of his soldiers, Alexander died.

Alexander had told his generals,
"When my casket is being
carried to the grave, leave
my hands hanging outside.
For empty-handed, I came into
this world and empty-handed, I
shall go! My whole life has been a
hollow waste, a futile exercise, for
no one at death can take anything
with them!"

In his brief lifetime of thirty-two years and eight months, Alexander the Great conquered most of the known world of the ancient Greeks. Although he destroyed much of the culture of those he conquered, he brought Greek civilization to the Asians and Asian civilization to the Greeks.

And he did all of this in only twelve years!

BLACK SEA

THRACE

Pella
MACEDONIA

Epirus

GREECE

Delphi

Chaeronea

MEDITERRANEAN SEA

Battle of Granicus

Troy

Sardis

Ephesus
Miletus

Halicarnassus

Phaselis

ASIA MINOR

Gordium
Ancyra

Tarsus

Battle of Issus

Faysh
Khabur

Gaugamela

Arbela

EUPHRATES RIVER

TIGRIS RIVER

Sidon
Tyre

Baghdad

Babylon

Matruh (Paraetonium)

Alexandria

EGYPT

Siwa

Memphis

NILE RIVER

ARABIAN
PENINSULA

RED
SEA

ALEXANDER'S ROUTE

ARAL SEA

AMU DAR'YA

CASPIAN
SEA

ASIA

ARMENIA

JAXARTES RIVER

Alexandria Eschate

CHINA

Samarqand (Maracanda)

SOGDIANA

KASHMIR

GANDHARA

AMU DAR'YA (OXUS) RIVER

Zadracarta

Caspian
Gates

Mashhad

BACTRIA

Balkh
Mazari Sharif

HINDU KUSH

HIMALAYAS

Dir

Rhagae

Kabul

Taxila
Aornos

Peshawar

HYDASPES
RIVER

Ecbatana

Alexandria
Areion

Alexandria

Alexandria
Bucephalis

PERSIA

ACESINES RIVER

RAVI RIVER

Susa

Alexandria

BEAS RIVER

Qala-i-Kang

Alexandria

Persepolis

Pasargadae

INDUS RIVER

Alexandria

INDIA

Hormuz

Pura

Alexandria

GEDROSIA

PERSIAN GULF

ARABIAN SEA